CALL THE OFFSHORE GUYS

BUGS
TOO MANY
HONEY

CAN IT
WAIT TILL
MONDAY ?

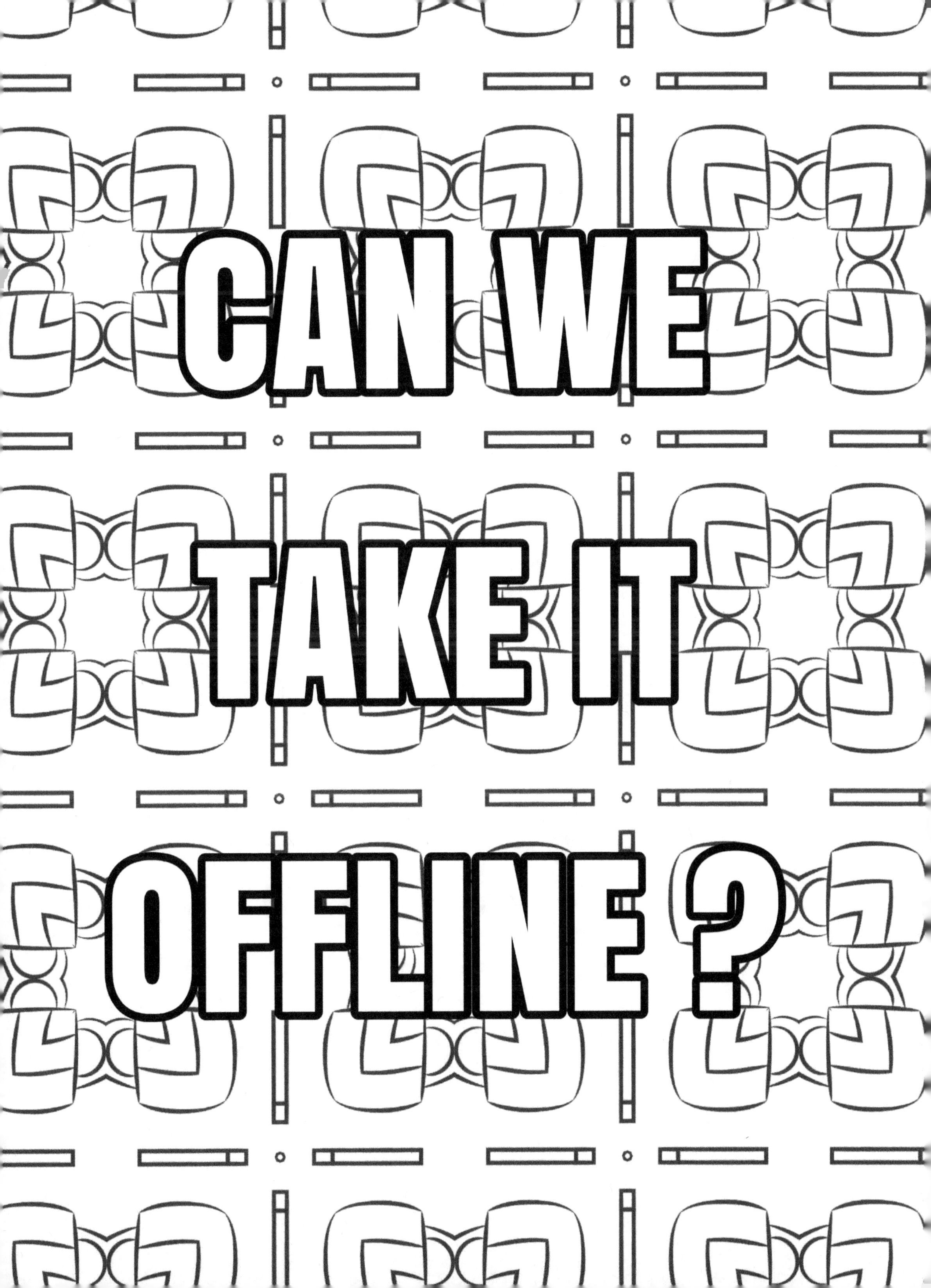
CAN WE
TAKE IT
OFFLINE ?

AIN'T A
TECH ISSUE
HUN

DEFER
TO NEXT
RELEASE

STAYING
BACK FOR
BEER ONLY

OUT OF SCOPE
NOT
HOPE

NAH
NOT A
DEFECT

WHY WASN'T
IT
PICKED UP ?

POKER
TIME
NOW

SCOPE CREEP
AND
WEEP

DRINKS
AFTER
RETRO

SPRINT TO

THE BAR

AFTER SPRINT

TEAM
BONDING THEN
ABSCONDING

WHERE'S
THE
SCRUMMASTER

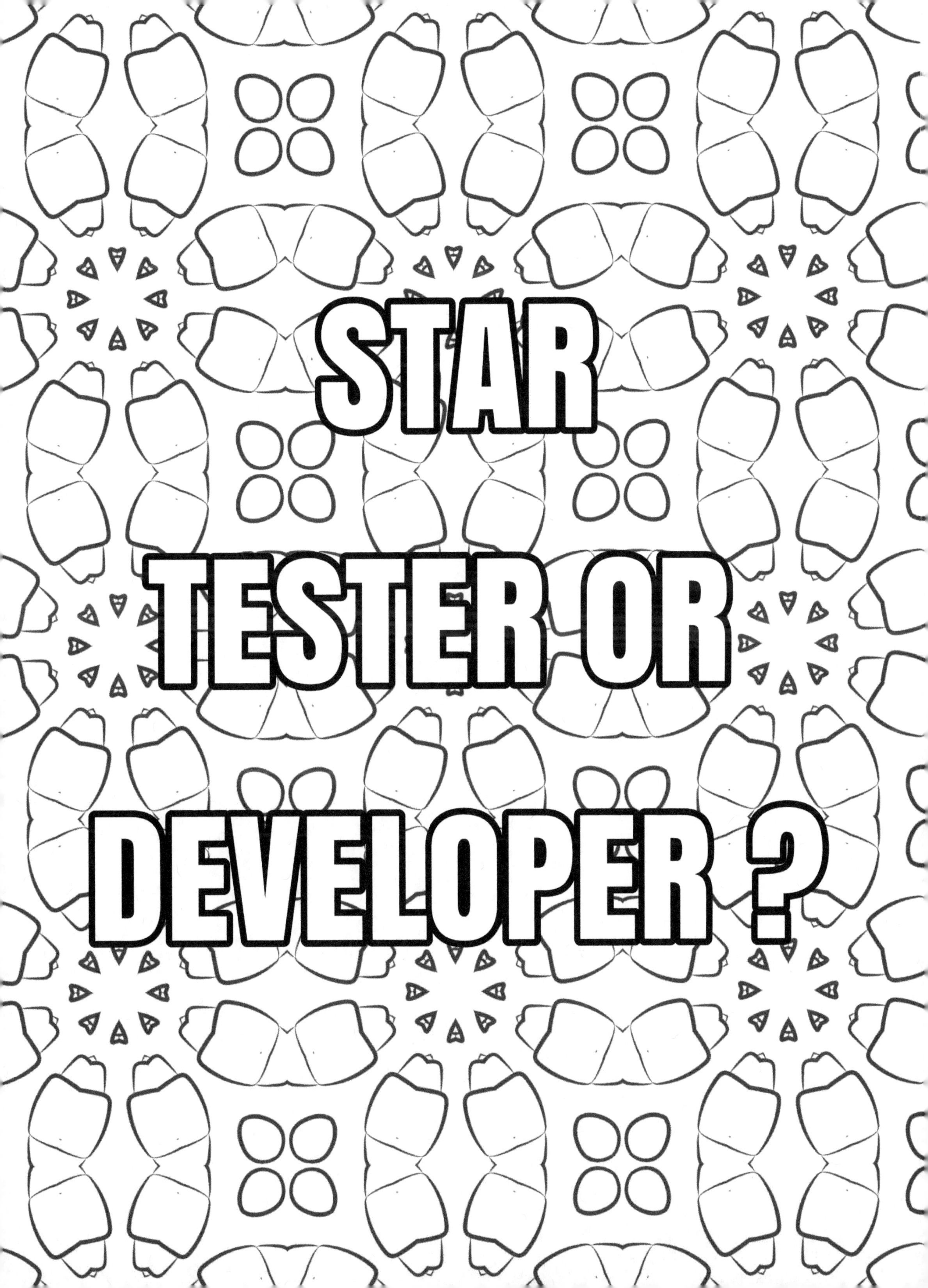
STAR
TESTER OR
DEVELOPER ?

www.ingramcontent.com/pod-product-compliance
Lightning Source LLC
LaVergne TN
LVHW081806050326
832903LV00027B/2113